Anxious in
a Sweet Store

Anna Jacobson

Anna Jacobson is an award-winning writer and artist from Meanjin (Brisbane). *Amnesia Findings* (UQP, 2019), her first full-length poetry collection, won the 2018 Thomas Shapcott Poetry Prize. In 2020 Anna won the Nillumbik Prize for Contemporary Writing and was awarded a Queensland Writers Fellowship. In 2018 she won the Queensland Premier's Young Publishers and Writers Award. Her poetry chapbook *The Last Postman* (Vagabond Press, 2018) was published as part of the deciBel 3 series. She was a finalist in the Brisbane Portrait Prize, Blake Art Prize, Olive Cotton Award, and Marie Ellis OAM Prize for Drawing. Her website is www. annajacobson.com.au.

Endorsements for *Anxious in a Sweet Store*

Unfolding tenderly and peppered with observational humour, *Anxious in a Sweet Store* is an intimate and insightful collection about the mind, about family, and about the beauty and complexity in daily life. Anna Jacobson lights up the dark. This gift of a book had me smiling and tearing up.

ELLEN VAN NEERVEN

There's no poet I know who can blend whimsy and catastrophe, casual visual eloquence and the gaps of memory loss, as persuasively as Anna Jacobson.

Anxious in a Sweet Store is disarmingly intimate and organic in its unaffected lyricism. Fearless in how it tackles medical and bureaucratic trauma, the poems also give ample space for celebrations of sweetness, dreams, the ballast of family, culture and poetry itself.

A bracing and grounding triumph.

ANDY JACKSON

If you spotted Anna Jacobson walking towards you, at a distance of say ... 200 metres, in a large, sloping public park, near dusk, you'd see three figures. In the centre, the self, to the left a stencil-dayglo outline, brimming with LED colour. To the right another stencil-dark outline, its gravity exquisitely tailored, silent, as it vacuums up remaining light. Now standing in front of you, smiling, still, those figures have merged into the singular presence Anna is. *Anxious in a Sweet Store* has its sugar trail but it's not always sweetness that lands on the tongue. Miniature torch on forehead, Anna sets off on a personal reconnaissance mission, cramming herself into vesicular spaces she is trying to escape from and find. Anna's antecedent aunts might well be Stevie Smith and Mirka Mora. Anna's words weigh themselves to the microgram. They analyse their handles with a Geiger counter for thought, the handles to open, the handles to let go, the handles to hang on to with the primary urge for survival. Anna's drawings absorb the ideas they float within, her index finger a direct nib. As a reader, you will find your own sighs in egg cartons. When Anna offers to pass 'the salt from my memory', put some on your own. Stay for a while. You might even find a pair of 'Corflute wings' in your top pocket, for heading home.

NATHAN SHEPHERDSON

In *Anxious in a Sweet Store*, Anna Jacobson shows us ways that people and objects play dress-ups to survive. These poems evoke music, mindfulness, muscle and imagination. They are levers, codes or keys, unlocking places with no answers, illuminating the strangeness of routine, the violence of compliance, and the necessity for consent. Ingredients can sing. Chairs can be unsupportive. Houses can sense. Roads can be rocky. The collection conjures both Yoko Ono's enchanting optimism and Samuel Beckett's existential I-can't-go-on-I'll-go-on. Anna dives into her memoir of memory loss, her eyes finding and naming, her hands collecting ticket stubs and deftly piecing her sweet particles together.

PASCALLE BURTON

I got anxious writing this endorsement, avoiding putting these words down. A sign that the work before me deeply matters, the poet behind the work matters more, that the poetry is living well beyond its immediate devices and constraints. People do die in seclusion rooms. Anxiety can manifest and monster. Reclaiming memory and medication from institutions comes at a cost. Few people can write into the heart and head of the mental health/illness lived experience with such shared generosity, clarity and tender offerings of the humanity and humour underneath it all. Singing cakes. Found childhoods. Where horn begins and piano ends. Crumbed fish and sharks, ocean and mind. There are seats within these poems. Choose one, take off the weight of what a poem should be, the weight of a life lived on others terms, rest here a while. Waiting in this collection's room is the wonder of waking life.

DAVID STAVANGER

Anna Jacobson

Anxious in a Sweet Store

With illustrations by Anna Jacobson

UPSWELL

First published in Australia in 2023
by Upswell Publishing
Perth, Western Australia
upswellpublishing.com

ISBN: 978-0-6455368-4-3

A catalogue record for this book is available from the National Library of Australia

NATIONAL LIBRARY OF AUSTRALIA

Cover design by Chil3, Fremantle
Typeset in Foundry Origin by Lasertype

Upswell Publishing is assisted by the State of Western Australia through its funding program for arts and culture.

Department of
**Local Government, Sport
and Cultural Industries**

GOVERNMENT OF
WESTERN AUSTRALIA

This book is dedicated to my brother, Alan

Contents

3. DREAM BLOCK

4. MEMORY CURLS

my mind
fizz bang sherbet
on the tongue

LIQUORICE ALLSORTS

Anxious in a Sweet Store

Footprint gummies

Signs confirm our fear: *be careful – what you take*
must be paid for. We do laps – imagine
the store's contents emptying
into our buckets by mistake. The guy
at the counter has run
the store since we were kids. We imagine
his disbelief – we are uninitiated
in the ways of self-serve. Our circling
complete, we leave – too nervous
to stop at the bargain bin. We walk
through the shopping centre, gummi-less.

Sour Gummi Worms

My pot was chives, yours
basil. Yours sprouted first, though
 I was older. I picked
out your seedlings when no one
was looking. Got in trouble
when Mum guessed what I'd done.
Five days later? Chives. I felt worse
than the big blue worm I'd accidentally
severed, while digging for dirt.

I've never been able to look after outdoor
plants. When I move out, my housewarming
gifts – all plants: aloe vera for burns,
geraniums (difficult to kill), a hardy plant with purple
flowers. The hardy plant is the first
to go, leaves shrivel, whispered dry
by wind. Geraniums crawl

with ants. Aloe vera turns
red in shock.

Back at our family home, you are now keeper
of the herb and veggie patch. You buy
special cloth to keep possums at bay. Your herbs
and plants flourish as though remembering
the old story. Plant-karma.

Friendship-ring gummies

One family holiday in Noosa
we made a secret language.
I wrote the code on two pieces of paper –
one copy each. Two decades later I've lost
the code. We still have our language –
know what the other is feeling or means
without words.

Gummi bears

We had twin beanbag animals:
mine with green-beaded eyes, yours
with blue, twin wooden rabbits: mine
hand-painted apricot, yours
blue. A banana
in pyjamas – I was B1 you
B2. Twin boxes filled
with frog-song: mine red yours
green. Dad brought back twin
Mickey Mouse clocks from a work trip.
We have twin Winnie-the-Poohs, one
cool yellow, one warm yellow, matching
red felt shirts. I have both.

For your 28th birthday I revisit
the sweet store, ask how to use
the self-serve. I gather
over a kilo of gummies. Footprint,
cherry, strawberry, Lego, friendship-ring,
sour gummi worms, cola, gummi bears.
We agree the clear ones are the best.

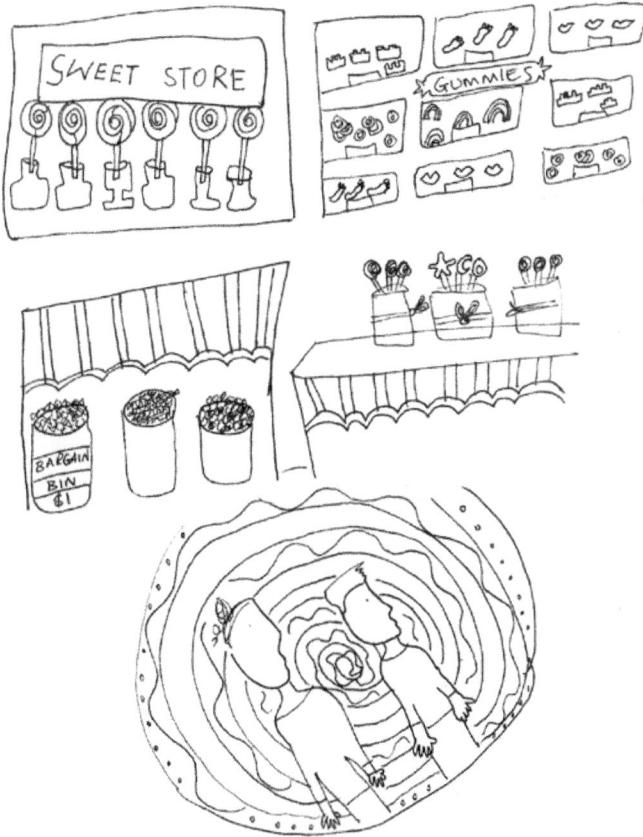

Cake Music

Honey sun and liquorice night, I pick   sky the colour of stomachache. I shelter
sugary stars and moon cake, hide   in the bakery – take a challah I baked
Allsorts in piano seats, sit   The baker unfurls
in pools of taffy-light,   in darkness, unable to ice the last
musk-dust motes turn   of the cakes. Oven ticks. We listen
star-anise-dark   to cakes' music: their crackle as they cook
in tins.   We can hear them sing.

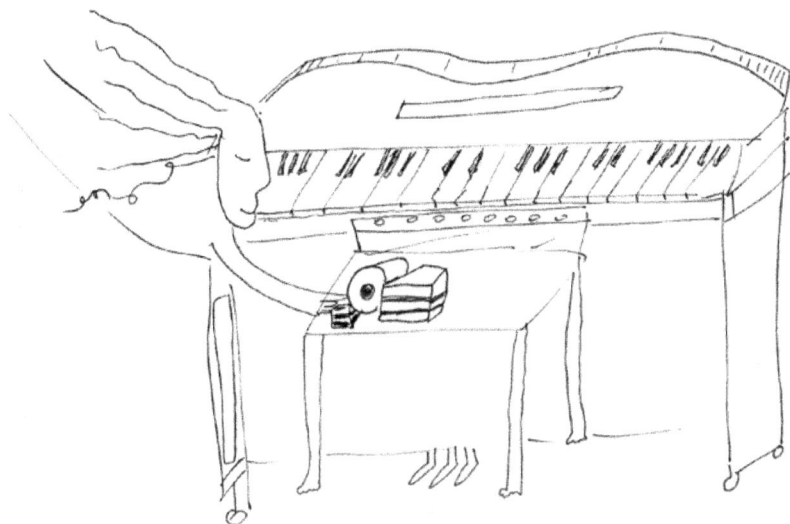

Suite in F

1.
I peer over concert
hall seats. My five-year-old eyes
caramelise on curly gold.
Everyone loves the harp, me –
the horns.

2.
The room is all shrieks
and sound-wisps. A single reed
for students, dipped into cups
of disinfectant. Tastes
like chemicals. I'm ten – can't get a sound
from a clarinet. Nor flute. In the middle
of the room – curly gold. Bypass
percussion, trombone, trumpets.
No one can get a sound out. I join
lines, place my lips against the mouthpiece,
the instrument emits a muffled honk;
the teacher sits up straighter. *That's a G.*
Try an F. I make another honk.

3.
Mazes of golden tubing against
indigo velvet-lined case. My parents
look dubious. *It's the same size as you.*
People say the French horn is the hardest
instrument to learn. I name
the loaned primary school horn *Goldie*.
The silver high-school horn *Moonshine*.
At seventeen my parents buy
me a second-hand horn. I call her
Mandy, after my adopted
cabbage-patch-doll.

4.
I needed air to fill my lungs. It was good
to be loud. I was the only horn player
in primary school. In high school
and beyond, horn players were drawn
together from our shared history of being
different. The horn section was for the quirky.
The French horn chose me. Became
my first voice.

5.
I join the Queensland Wind
Orchestra at the Old Museum Building.
Before and after rehearsals I take
my horn on adventures, visit
the old piano in the basement. I finally
find the bell-like tone of a French horn,
can sight-read, fingers press
the language of keys. I look
at the music, practice edging
my way forwards bar by bar, until I know
where piano ends and horn begins.

6.
I am 21 when my anxiety flares. I lose
stamina, stop practising. Thoughts
and doubts whisk
air from lungs. I can't play
for two-hour rehearsals, can't
hold the high notes. When I'm depressed
the instrument weighs
heavy, I can hardly lift
it, balance bell on knee. My meds
give me a lip tremor on low
notes, a constant vibrato. I'm forced
to stick to the middle register.

7.
When I quit the band, my playing
stops. Dreams start. Instead of oiling valves,
keys stick. Instead of greasing
slides, they fill with sand. I played
the French horn for fifteen
years. Over a decade of French horn
dreaming since I stopped.

8.
I tell people I used to play, still dream
about the horn – they want me
to pick it up again – tell me
it's my subconscious calling. I recognise
the roar from Tchaikovsky's Swan
Lake, the soaring opening music from BBC's
Narnia, the Jupiter in the Planets
by Holst. My favourite instrument is still
the French horn. I knew the sound
before I knew its name.

French horn with music-note sequins (detail)
Anna age 5

Echoic Memory

Zither calls
back
into the antique
shop. Rose
and leaf
motif
on lacquer
32
strings
like bright
boiled lollies
in waxy
paper placed
on
synagogue
benches,
for children
to throw
at the bar
mitzvah kid
I visit
three times
on my
twenty-eighth
birthday
I visit
again
the assistant
unlocks
glass
cabinet

zither
gifts echoic
memory akin
to an out-of-tune
grandfather
twanging
every quarter of
an hour
I run
my hand
over strings
a cat pounces
off key
pianos

including
broken
Howard
piano
painted
gold
on red
in the basement
of the Old
Museum
Building
sharp
keys
prized off
I pluck

the assistant
wraps
zither
in butcher's paper
says she feels
it's going
to a good
home
invites me
to busk
outside
their shop
once
I've learned
to play
I hear
zither strings
ping
by themselves
sense wood
breathing
as days
shrink
and expand
like the door
that doesn't wedge
shut
in summer
closes
perfectly
in winter

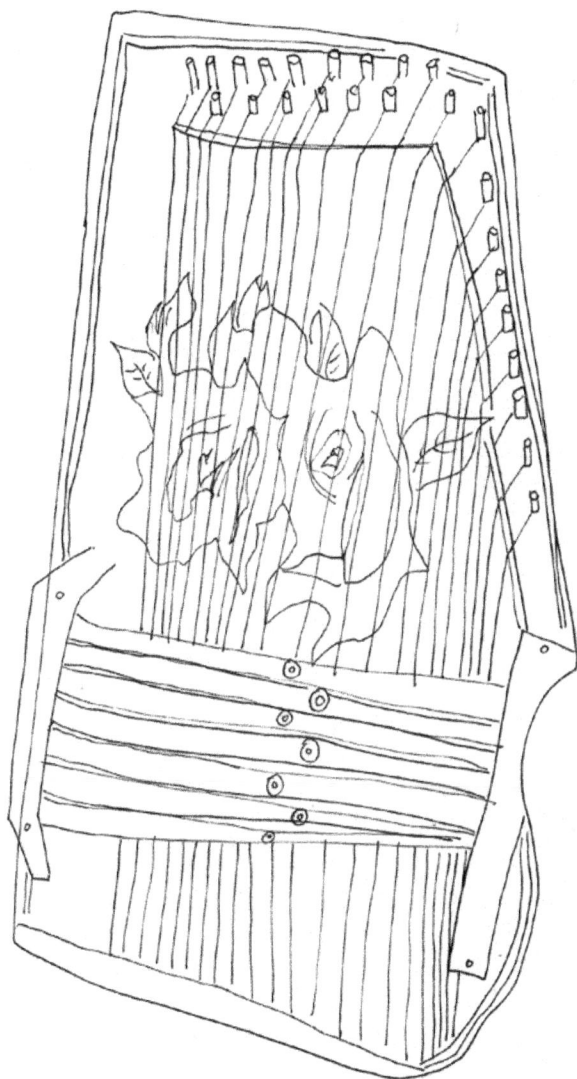

Row F Seat 10

I was a theatre usher – could seat two hundred people

CC   1 2 3 4 5 6 7 8 9 10 11 12 13 14 15 16 17 18 19 20 21 22 23 24 25   CC

through my door in the time it took to eat an ice cream.

BB   1 2 3 4 5 6 7 8 9 10 11 12 13 14 15 16 17 18 19 20 21 22 23 24 25   BB

I remembered each face, features vanishing afterwards

AA   1 2 3 4 5 6 7 8 9 10 11 12 13 14 15 16 17 18 19 20 21 22 23 24 25   AA

like my handful of ticket stubs. One stayed, caught

A   1 2 3 4 5 6 7 8 9 10 11 12 13 14 15 16 17 18 19 20 21 22 23   A

in the lining of my pocket: a woman, hands trembling

B   1 2 3 4 5 6 7 8 9 10 11 12 13 14 15 16 17 18 19 20 21 22 23 24   B

as though her ticket might rewrite itself to announce

C   1 2 3 4 5 6 7 8 9 10 11 12 13 14 15 16 17 18 19 20 21 22 23 24 25   C

the wrong day or play. I remembered her because time

D   1 2 3 4 5 6 7 8 9 10 11 12 13 14 15 16 17 18 19 20 21 22   D

had torn: I was both usher and this woman. Reassuring

E   1 2 3 4 5 6 7 8 9 10 11 12 13 14 15 16 17 18 19 20 21   E

a version of myself.

F   1 2 3 4 5 6 7 8 9 10 11   F

Lucky Monday

I buy a tall vase
small mouth
to sing
to my lucky bamboo.
At home I glimpse
a sticker stuck to the pot *this item*
is made from porous materials, do not
fill with water. I put my vase
that is not a vase aside. I order a glass
vase online. I have the usual anxious
thoughts – they won't let me return
the non-vase. The glass vase will smash
in the post and I'll be forever trying
to find a home for my lucky bamboo
that won't apply luck
to its own pot.

Upon Accidentally Walking into an Upmarket Sushi Restaurant with My Hungry Brother

Mineral or sparkling? Tap,
please. Two iced jugs. Alone
in the restaurant classical
music discording unease, we open
the menu: four pieces of sushi: $14.
Rolls? No, pieces.

It's six times the cost of what I pay
at the mall. We've been mistaken
for emperors wanting the fabled
kind, made by experts in the art
of sashimi. I take in the silver, heavy
cloth across my lap, no
loose threads to unravel
the situation. The waitress waits
for our order. I look
at my brother. *We have to go now,* he says.
As we scamper, hands
appear from behind
plastic trees, whip
away napkins, remove
glasses, change
the place settings as though we
were never there.

Dad and Led Zeppelin

My brother finds a safe disguised
in a book. Plastic brown cover: spin
the wheel three times past zero,
turn right until 19, left until 8, slide
and pull. Inside is the gold
we are after – photos
of Dad with 70s-wild hair,
from his student union cards
and hostel backpacking days.
If only all family clues came
with codes.

Dad looks at our discovery. Flips
through stamps on his hostel passport.
They made me cut my hair
in Singapore, he says.
I search *long hair, 70s, Singapore*,
discover Operation Snip Snip –
a ban on long hair. Barber stalls set up
at checkpoints. Visitors turned away
at immigration if they did not comply
with a quick trim. Led Zeppelin refused,
tour plans
          cut
short.

Suggestible House

1.
I boil the kettle, pour hot
water into the sunflower
cup, hear a crack, feel heat
splash my feet. The cup has split,
each half stands
as though wet clay sliced
by taut fishing line.
The house can sense
your stress my brother says.
In another room,
the doorknob
                falls off
in my father's hand.

2.
My mother's solution to my anxiety:
blue-tack removal. My room once housed
a gallery: concert and bus tickets, opening-
night art, postcards, photographs, a sea-
horse swizzle stick. I peel
off two decades by hand. Try
the blunt edge of a butter
knife, a paint scraper. My mood creates perfect
blue-tack removal conditions. The whole
room done in an hour.

3.
My father watches a horror film at 3am:
creatures claw to the ground above. The tiles
in our family room are old – humidity
and moisture make them shift,
crack, groan. My mother discovers my father
perched on chair's edge, surrounded by lifting
tile shards.

ROCKY ROAD

Concerns Before Attending a 4-Week Anxiety Program

↔ Getting there
     "   "   on time
Scoping the exits
Being in a room full of anxious people
  "   "   "   "   " in a hospital

Having lunch
Coming in late from lunch
Being mistaken for an inpatient
  "   institutionalised for extreme levels of anxiety

Having a panic attack
  "   "   " when being taught how to breathe,
  "   "   "   "   "   "   "   " causing
the other day patients
            to
               p
                a
               n
                i
               c

∞ Getting there

Day-patient Mindfulness

1.
Our backs press
        earth. I suspend
                clouds, catch
                        leaves and bird-
                                song, brush
                    grass. I close
                        my eyes – trains
                                    are oceans.

2.
After infinity or 10 min, Nurse says
    Let's drink tea mindfully. Café
    noise exhausts. Nurse's lanyard
    a siren. Can people tell?
    Does she come here
with patients every day? Milkshakes
expensive as a meal, I think sideways

into another cabinet –
raspberry
ices the doughnut. Focus
on crunchy cinnamon sugar –
Nurse looks up
from first sip – *it was there
a minute ago*,

or was it ever there?

I'm efficient
at this mindfulness business.

Scattering Matter

                               I

                    I   I
                         s
              I   I   I
         I   I   I   I
      I   I   I   I
         I   I   I   I   I   I
            II   I am made from scattering matter I
   I   I   try to keep hold of my particles I   I   I g
         II I   I   email my psychiatrist. I   I
       n I   take my ineffective meds I   I c a
               I   rate my mood as *very bad* I
   I   I   I   I.   am tethered to outer space – I   I   I
               I   am stuck in a dark poem I
                          am scattering I
         I   I   II   I   I   I   I   t   I   I
      I   I   I   I   I   I   I   I   I   I
                         I   I
                    t   I
         I   I   c   I   I
            I   I   I   I.

            .   .   .

                    .   a   .

                    .   .

                    .   t   .
                         I

Your Updated DSM Diagnosis

Cycloid
      cyclops
            cyclone(d) –

you left your body, floated
with the consciousness of coma.
Psychosis diagnosis
beyond the DSM –

Your body did whatever it did.
                People did things to it –
                you do not know what –
                you were not there.

Electric storms convulsed. Cyclones
banished memory to another realm.

Anxiety in its place.

People Die in Seclusion Rooms

Woman covered face to feet
under a white sheet on a bare
concrete floor in a bare
concrete room.

Walls say: *Another one.*

Woman is dead, the staff
did not watch. No one wants to
watch a woman who cannot watch
for herself.

Walls say: *We are the watchwomen.*

She fell many times and hit
her head on a bare concrete floor
in a bare concrete room. That woman
could have been me.

What do you want, padded walls? says Nurse.

Walls say: *We want all soft edges and no room.*

Doc looks me in the eyes.
You were placed in seclusion
many times, more than most.
Do you remember this?

No, I don't remember.

I was not there in my self while my body
lay on the bare mattress and screamed
for my return.

Nurses made brief records – un-watching
the woman who cannot watch for herself.

Hospital file tells me I smuggled
in a pen. Security assisted. The pen
was removed. I wrote on the floor with cold
cups of tea. My words were not noted –
no one wants to listen to the woman
who cannot hear herself.

They removed the bedframe in case
I hit my head. But what of the bare concrete
floor in a bare concrete room filled
with ghosts of those from before?

I don't remember the seclusion room.
Though a part of my self still haunts
its walls, floor, page.

It's Been a Decade Since I Went Mad

Word-finding difficulties when I had world-
finding difficulties. I tried to escape
through the ward door laced
with three nurse-sharks. My escape-
route lives as a fish-hook scar on my ring
finger, forever wanting to reel me back.
I have cut the line loose – hook remains
in slammed skin, alerting doctors
wielding metal detectors every blue-sinker
moon. Nurse-sharks wrote I smashed fire
alarms – my mind *was* fire. But the electric
eel will always find you. They put out the fire
from their freshwater asylum, preserved themselves
in the salt of my missing memory.

Fish Walk

On Tuesdays I walk to get fish. I call it my 'fish walk'. My Doc says people who eat fish have better mental health. So I get fish and chips on Tuesdays to keep up with the fish-eating-happy-people my Doc says are out there. All the animals in the street follow me on my fish walk. Either they are drawn to my sadness or can smell the promise of soon-to-be-bought fish. I do not like fish but will eat it crumbed with chips and lemon. On my fish walk I pass pumpkins and their yellow flowers growing down a hilltop. I pass plums on the footpath. I pass books for sale in a fruit box. I could catch the train, but then it would not be my fish walk. The people on the train do not care if tears track my face, do not ask if I am okay – I prefer the animals with their innate sense. I prefer my fish walk, even though I do not like fish.

When Does the Strange Lady Leave?

My antidepressant stops working. Acute
anxiety unleashed. I need to reacquaint
myself with a hospital. My doctor
recoils. I ask – *giant spider? No,
a cockroach, would it upset you
if I kill it?* It climbs through patients'
files 124–698 from 2020. She squishes
the roach in her fingers
with a tissue.

I want to time the hospitalisation.
I'm a bridesmaid. The roach crawls
from bin to floor powering prehistoric
energy. She stomps on it five times. *I think
that can be arranged.* I buy my family four
vanilla-custard doughnuts to break
the news.

Gardenias leak tears from hidden
cracks. A plant cutting from Mum, to keep
until admission. My bro drives
me to the chemist. We get stuck
behind a bus that asks *R U OK?*
to the lyrics of *everything's gonna
be alright.*

The previous day my bro asked
my parents: *when does the strange lady
leave?* Today we make dinner together.
I put oranges in a salad and sauté
onions, forget to cry.

Pissing in the ECT Rooms at the End of 2020

My nurse
wants
a urine
sample, can't
find
bottles,
takes me
to
the electroconvulsive therapy rooms.
In the drawer –
a tray. I piss
up a storm, tray
overflows drenches undies. I hold my piss in hand, worried they'll
think I'm here for ECT. Nurse returns, dips strip in piss, says: *not bad
at all*, pours piss down sink. We both wash our hands –
she, of my piss. Me, of this room.

Grounding Techniques

Where are your feet?
They twitch in a bed.

Where are your hands?
They type this poem on a phone
in the dark, at 5.49pm.

Where is your psychiatrist?
Boxed in an office.
She once said I have a straight
face some would call 'resting
bitch face'. She said to practise
smiling in the mirror. I did not practise
but left her practice after 9 years
of similar asides.

Where is your psychologist?
Stewing in a field of citrus. She tells me
to suck on lemons. *You suck
on a lemon.* She says to acknowledge
my anger. *It's acknowledged,* I say – *now what?*
But time's up and that's for next session.

Where is your fun?
My life is a pandemic, and my brain
is on fire withdrawing
from an antidepressant that tried
to kill me. Fun is quarantined
in this realm.

Where is your stomach?
It's big and round, right here, filled
with ten years of antipsychotics.

Where are your lungs?
I put them away in a drawer.
They don't work at night.

Where is your lockdown?
In a room with an indoor plant
that has twenty-one leaves. The leaves   .
continue to unfurl while I stagnate
in their water tray.

Where are your eyes?
They are wet and held in the crook
of my elbow, which I sometimes use
to open train doors.

Where is your God?
In the wrong dress pocket, somewhere
in my cupboard.

Where is your brain?
Lost in a fog.

Where is your heart?
A long way from home.

If I Were Made of Copper

I would not age well. Turquoise forming –
not lyrical veins down my body, meaningfully
etched, but bulbous corrosion at every joint.
No healing properties for me. Each morning I wake
a statue. Walk through the day a statue. Turquoise tears
etched on coppery face, collecting at edges
of chin, elbows, eyes. I corrode corrode
corrode. Therapists want to saw me off
at the head. Therapists say: *drink this formula,*
this graph, this table, let me shine
lights in your eyes to heal your complex
trauma. My metal refuses to polish. I leave
the therapists. Drag my crying sawn-off head
through streets. Therapists say: *I will close*
my file on you. What they really say:
you can lead a horse to water, but you can't
make her drink. No, you can't make me drink
from poisoned pastel lagoons. Let me run,
run, run.

Instead of Walking Alone I Join a Walking Group

Walk 1

We meet at Confucius
in the South Bank herb
garden. I sit near a potted
pomegranate tree, watch
moorhens moor
by water features.

One hundred fairy lights entwine
Moreton Bay Figs near Goodwill
Bridge. Each branch holds
rising moons.

Walk 2

No two walks are the same. We pass
climbers at Kangaroo Point cliffs. We walk
through our designated hour. A ferry arcs
us back across the river. I get
my walking badge.

Walk 3

We arrive at Roma Street gardens, rain
cooling sweat from skin. Water
dragon heads tilt as we dart
through rainforest canopies lit
with ibis. Below, flowers pop purple:
mauve, lilac, violet, galaxy, presented
as a birthday cake sculpture at golden
hour. The parklands are turning 20.

In this dusked realm I believe
there's magic in wishes, spells
in nature, incantations in walking.

Walk 4

The Brisbane River folds
me into mangrove
worlds. I start to feel
better. I know this is true,
because I can finally write
a poem not sorrow-drowned. For now –
until next full moon, I can see
the stars.

Lessons in Anxiety

1.
Before a big day accept and acknowledge
anxiety – like a barometer measuring
atmospheric pressure with mercury, water,

                                                    air.

2.
Assure yourself it won't be the end
of the world. You've already
been there. You've seen it for what it is. Stood
on its edge. And you survived. If
it is the end, you'll deal with it then.

3.
Now go to the park.
Unbutton sky. This is your home-
work.

4.
Practise for 10 minutes each day.

5.
Things will get better, I promise.

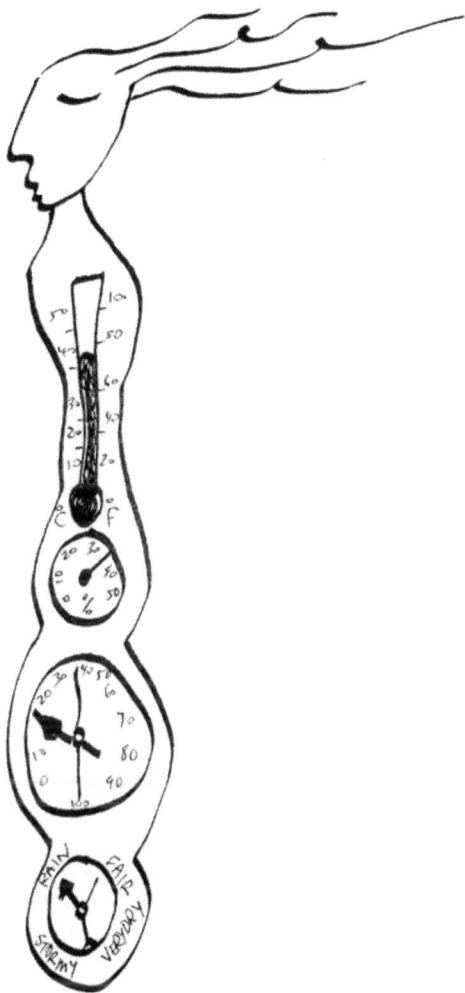

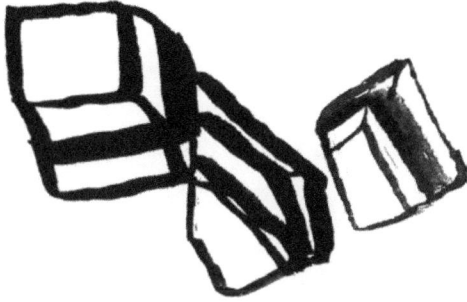

DREAM BLOCK

Good Night Sleep Tight and Don't Mind the Fox

The sleep-lady asks me to draw my dreams –
sketch dogs who have bitten off my hands.
Bright textas float above sharp paper reams.

Draw the fox who shadows rooms' stretching seams –
dread absent, in marker's rainbow bands,
the sleep-lady asks me to draw my dreams.

She tells me to look at a dollhouse, beams –
I don't have one at home, my hope expands.
Bright textas float above sharp paper reams.

Her dollhouse has no pots for sauces, creams,
no pantry filled with jars of hundreds and thousands.
The sleep-lady asks me to draw my dreams.

Put the dolls to bed, she says, but this means
my wooden peg doll is alone, no arms or hands.
Bright textas float above sharp paper reams.

The dolls dream cardboard-colours, nothing gleams.
I'm making my parents sick with demands
says the sleep-lady, who asks me to draw my dreams.
Bright textas float above sharp paper reams.

Code Cracker

1.
When the forest calls, she befriends
trees. Decodes the scribbly gum in half
an hour. She is taken away, trees' voices
muffled through hospital balcony bars.

After six weeks she can no longer
hear them. No longer remember
the secret language she'd learned
from the scribbly gum moth.
When doctors show her a picture
of bark she cannot decipher,
    they l
        e
            t
                her
                go.

2.
Our lemon tree is fruiting.
    We have too many.
I thank her, peer
            inside; four   lemons   the size of grapefruit.
My mother bakes fish with   lemon   and dill.
            I make a   lemon   tart sans short-crust base.
            Communal   lemon   in the fridge for cups of tea:
                               lemon   and honey,
                        lemon   and ginger,
                    lemon   and mint.
        The last   lemon   waits in the fruit bowl
to become zest, sliced into quarters,
squeezed, or preserved. Instead, I sit
at the table, ink and paper, draw
it whole. I draw until it becomes

something Other. I draw
its talk. Stippled as a weathered ear, it listens
to my pen on paper, bushels
me stories. From the lemon I draw
the tree. From the tree I draw
the sky. From the sky I draw
the scribbly gum moth.

Centrelink Suite – Tales from a NewStart

Prove It

*A forty-five-minute assessment to prove
you still have a mental illness.* I show
him the letter from my psychiatrist.
*Doctors' letters are only valid short-term
at Centrelink.* I cry until the security
guard meanders. *Can I help you
with anything else?* At a café I order
the special: double-glazed caramel
popcorn, churros, ice cream with fudge
sauce. I text Mum:

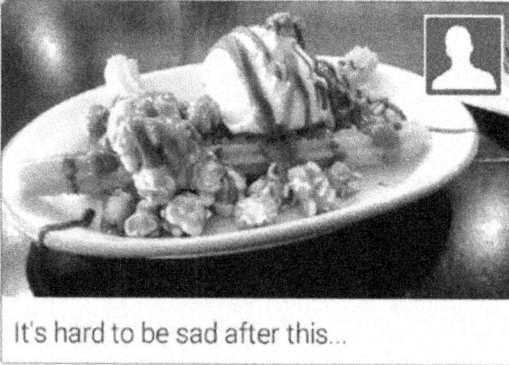

It's hard to be sad after this...

3 May

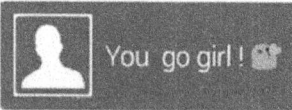

You go girl!

3 May

How my Centrelink provider helps me prep for a job interview

The day before my job interview
my Centrelink provider makes me attend
a two-hour job search. I fill
forms requiring complicated passwords: 8-16
characters long, upper case and numerals, just
in case someone logs in and steals
my resumé. The form asks:
Do I have a medical condition?
I tick yes. *Does it require routine medication?*
I tick yes.
Do I have any of the following?
I tick anxiety and depression. The squares
onscreen deflate. I want to prep
for my job interview. I text
my mother who says: *Don't let the bastards
get you down. Write a poem.* I write
down the names of jobs that inspire
my senses: *popcorn maker, cheese
specialist.* After two-hours I am exhausted
from sitting in chairs as unsupportive
as the staff. My case manager wishes
me good luck with my interview.
Get some rest, she says.

*How my Centrelink provider rings me
during a psychiatrist appointment to make sure
I am there*

I have a psychiatry appointment during
my two-hour monitored job search. I've told
my provider this many times. Even rang
the day before, so they don't forget. If they don't
verify I have a valid reason for not attending
the job search, I'll go into the warning
zone. As my psychiatrist is finding

ways to help my mood through self-
care, my phone rings. *Hi Anna,*
it's your Centrelink provider – how are you?
I'm in my psychiatrist appointment.
Okay I was just calling to check that was where
you actually were. I hang up. Luckily,
I can get therapy for that call right now.

On Streets Named After Royalty

Central Station – Corner of Ann and Edward Street

On the train someone hands
a man a dollar. *Thanks brother.*
When I catch a fish, I'll give it to you.
I set the man by the sea; he hooks
fish upon fish. I place the other man
by the shore. The man sees him, offers
the fish. The doors open,
I get off the train – leave them
to their conversation, leave them
to their feast.

George Street

At a café, I sit next to a man
in oversized suit jacket stained
ocean green. He eats meringue
bent over, uses his fingers
to scoop up the cream. He pulls
out a magnifying glass to read
the newspaper. A waitress bustles
past. He startles, *I'm just reading*
the paper before realising
she's serving someone else. He isn't
doing anything wrong, she isn't
asking him to leave.

Queen Street Mall

She unfurls her anemone palm
showing fish-scale rows
of twenty cent pieces. She's followed
me from George Street, *I'm doing it tough,*

livin' on the streets. Can you lend me three
or four dollars for some food?
Peak hour crowds swim in summer,
her shoulders hunch in a grey jumper.
I open my wallet – add gold and silver.
God bless you, darl, she disappears
in the current. I turn left at the fountain,
recycled water and dirty ibis, drift
across Adelaide Street to my bus stop, wonder
what will happen to her, wonder
what she will eat.

Royal Brisbane and Women's Hospital Bus Interchange

The floral cup moves closer to smashing
on the floor, hooked on his finger all the way
from King George Square. Characters shoal
the platform. *I was once you, may yet*
be you again. I suppose these thoughts
are to be expected when you live one stop
from your old psychiatric hospital, one stop
from mind's circling fins.

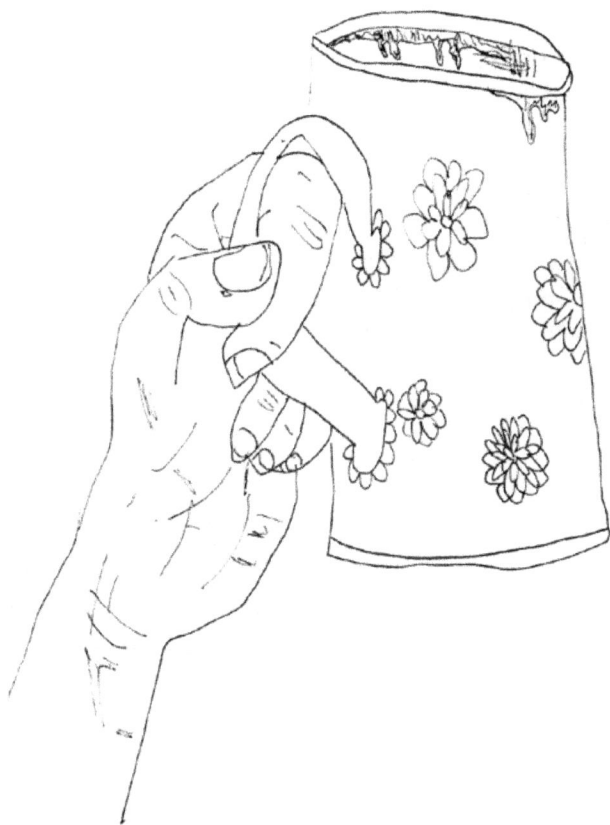

Profiling

I am told to list my skills.
I type *writer* and *artist*.
Based on my responses, according
to my Centrelink provider, I am
most suited to being a security guard
or aviation protection officer.
I had no idea keywords
such as *writer* and *artist* could evoke
such muscle.

When I am stopped
at airport security I'd like to think
it's my indigo sequins –
too much bling? But I am wrong –
they've just heard from Centrelink
and want to meet their future colleague.

How I Didn't Get the X-ray Filing Job

I applied because of my experience
as a theatre usher, could find row 'H'
in the dark – knew it came before 'I'
and after 'G', without a torch.

I applied because I thought filing X-rays
in a backroom sounded
soothing. The hush-swish
of folders. More comfortable with bone-
whispers.

The more anxious I get, the more brightly
I dress. The interview was doomed
from the start – I tried to be corporate – found
a jacket from an op shop – peach – went fabulously
with my purple skirt trimmed
in rainbow.

I'd missed the memo to dress
in theme – X-ray black-and-white with hints
of swirling grey. Or perhaps a chiffon top the colour
of manila folder. Knowing the alphabet in order
was not enough, I had to dress like an X-ray, inhabit
the X-ray, be the X-ray. I didn't get the job.

Time for an Adventure

A staircase leading 126 flights
from garage to ocean. A parcel
with a key – instructions: *take this
to the front desk.* I do not want
this quest filled
with other peoples' wants, though
in a dream people say
every character is you.

Dolphin Treats

During pandemics, dolphins bring gifts ~
sea-treasures to lure disappearing humans ~
barnacled bottles, coral, sponges.

For the promise of feeding-time cod, dolphins wash
ashore King Neptune's crown ~ for a toss
of tuna, they spit out pirate-gold from underwater
caves ~ for a taste of herring, they nose
their way through shipwrecks for pearls
in oysters and clams.

Dolphins are intelligent ~
they know humans have bleached
the reef ~ for future mackerel delights
they carry lumps of white.

I Can Feel Lonely Opening a Can of Tuna

1.
I'm so lonely I type *lonely*
into Google. One site says
loneliness is as bad
for your health as smoking
15 cigarettes a day. I guess
I'll die soon.

2.
Government Covid19 restrictions lift;
loneliness seeps my eyelids, plays
with tear ducts. I muffle
sobs so hard I give
myself a sore throat. Will I need
to be tested?

3.
Self-restrictions have
not lifted. My anxiety makes sure
of it. You can have 20 people over
to your house and I am yet to see
a single friend.

4.
My brother saw an echidna
on his walk. Second time
in twenty-years. I missed
the sighting, was back at home unable
to make myself go outside.

5.
Google says creativity helps
loneliness so I wrote this poem.

6.
I can feel lonely in a packed room. I can
feel lonely when restrictions lift. I can feel
lonely opening a 425g can of tuna serving
four people.

7.
Seven is a lucky number. Seven
is a spell, a ritual, an incantation. I write
down seven things to banish loneliness: baking,
walking, dance classes, sketching, writing,
photos, Zoom with my friends.

Pilates for the Depressed

Oblique asks if we have injuries
she should know about. She doesn't ask *why
are you here?* so I do not answer:
for my depression. We fold
our bodies in half. Strengthen
our core. The more hardcore
the teacher, the more
we check our watches. *Let your face relax
and turn to candle wax, dripping
to the floor.* Casper

is into horror. *Last week those candleholders
exploded glass all over the studio – the work
of ghosts.* I scan the floor for stray
shards near bare feet. Peaches

uses food metaphors. In winter:
*imagine balancing a hot bowl of soup on your back
and hot cups of cocoa on your knees – don't
let them tip! Rest giant marshmallows under
your hands. Balance an orange beneath
your chin.* We become mermaids and super-
women. Dolphins and butterflies. Rose

has us lie with closed eyes on our mats –
at the end of the class she rubs
perfume against her hands, presses
the scent into each of our shoulders. We leave
smelling of luxe bubble gum.

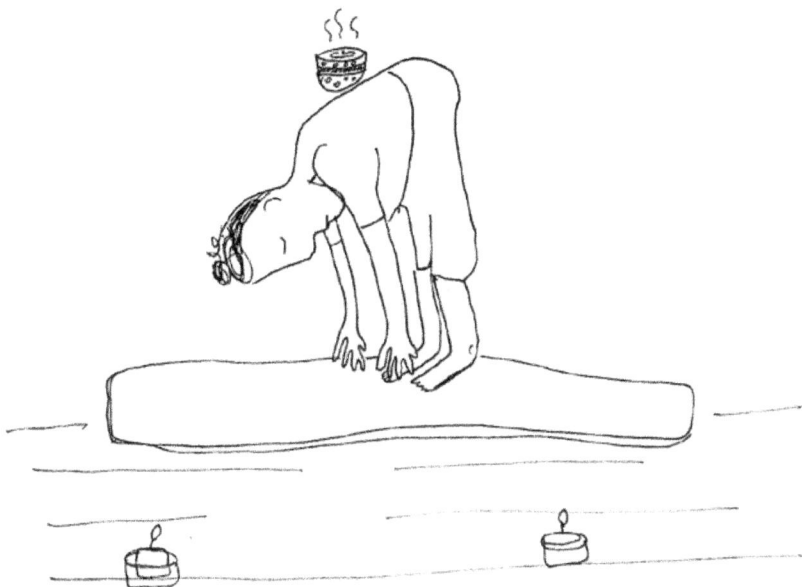

Offerings

I have dreams where lower molars wobble.
I twist them, fingers paint with tooth-blood –
realise the next one is loose and the next.
I pull them all out in ceremony, tooth-offerings
placed on sink's porcelain edge. My mother says
it's an anxiety dream, or fear of old age.
My brother says teeth are linked to power.
My father doesn't remember his dreams.

I leave keys in my dreams, as though I will return later to collect them. I leave them in places only I know where to find them: the closed mouth of a felt doll handstitched by my great grandmother in an existential third bedroom at my share-house I haven't noticed before; a key in a pale pink ballet shoe I hide beneath the trapdoor that leads to the theatre where the performance will take place. Sometimes a key is delivered back to me in a paper package with a message to take it to the twenty-fifth stair above sea-level. Some keys must be scattered over ground, so that in emergencies, the dreamer will find at least one. But some dreams don't need keys. They need levers. Levers that can be pushed.

Dreams During a Pandemic #1

31 March 2020

The entire Jewish community is here. I ask my uncle what's going on. He tells me – I can't hear over the sound of large trucks on train tracks, filled with my people. I try to find the lever to release trucks from tracks. A train is coming. Mum is at the park by the tracks – we keep being separated. No matter how hard we try to stay together, we are being pushed, onwards.

Dreams During a Pandemic #2

2 April 2020

I stand with my mother by an enclosure. I don't
want to look inside. I know all the butterflies
in the butterfly-house are dead or fluttering
low to the ground. The birds are breathing
heavily – plumage expanding – exotic, not used
to this heat. My mother stands too close
to the enclosure – the largest blue
Macaw sticks its beak through wires, near
her face. *Mum, stand back.*
They've put bats in there as well, she says,
too devastated by the destruction
of these creatures to hear
my warning.

Dreams During a Pandemic #3

5 April 2020

My eyes are charted
by an astronomer. The bigger
my eyes, the more lethargic
I will feel. The results
come back – my moon
eyes take up the page. I accidentally
forward my eyes to my friend
in an email. I am too exhausted
to care.

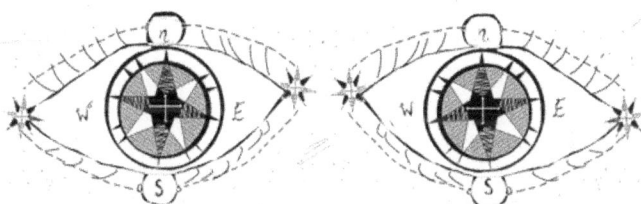

One of These Scenes is Not Real

A man frankensteins through the bus aisle, hands
held out like red boiled crabs. Teen girls laugh
as he lurches past. I understand why he can't
touch rails – understand something terrible would happen
to his life, loved ones, the bus and people on it.

When I was ten I flicked light switches. If I didn't
complete the ritual, something bad would happen.
I dreaded being asked to switch
off the lights for the projector in grade four – knew
I'd have to complete the on-off on-off on-off,
in various sequences, not able
to stop until it felt right.

I driftwood through jobs, beach myself
in debris. Stranded I navigate to shore, battle
waves for my Round-the-Twist accommodation. I shell
out peas for payment at dinner time. But Bronson
doesn't want peas, he wants to read my comic
Fart Girl and the Chemist Crush to keep
the lighthouse ghosts at bay. I tell him
I've only made part 1 and 2. That's all
he wants.

When I get depressed, I draw my face. Sometimes
I don't have strength to lift
the pen but on nights where strange energy combusts,
I do. *Self-Portrait While Depressed* is a series of nine
drawings over a thirty-minute period. I enter
it into a drawing prize. I live off prize money,
I apply, apply, apply. I discover
I am a finalist in the drawing prize.

I answer the phone as though a serial killer
is on the other line. It's the framers.
Can I pick it up another day?
Yes, that's fine.
I'm sure the framer understands
my nerves, having just affixed nine
of my *self-portrait while depressed* drawings
behind glass. Surely he is well-versed in the cycle
of anxiety to depression to anxiety, though one
cannot make assumptions. When I pick
up my work, the framer will point
to the drawings and say: *hey, it's you.*

Do dreams count as reality? If you have dreamt
something and remember it, the dream
becomes a memory; something real to the dreamer.
One thing I know for sure: I like to find
the unusual in the everyday, until the everyday
becomes unusual. This is a nonfiction poem. But one
of these scenes is not real.

MEMORY CURLS

Ingredients for Preservation

Wear calico dress with blue board
shoes, Corflute wings, Mylar
glasses, dangling
Ethafoam earrings. Create
houses for each object. Know
what is inside without reference image.
Bundle up rust from your great-great-uncle's
chandelier, each bulb, the light itself. Take
care with the light, it has a habit
of sneaking out again. Use double
layers if necessary. Worry
about which object you might ruin next
with your care. Like your great-
grandmother's dinner set and plates –
the kind that makes eating
chicken soup a silky experience.
Lick the porcelain. Taste
the gold, before wrapping
in Tyvek – not too tightly or the handles
may snap. Best not to unwrap again.

Offer to preserve others' objects.
Become outcast, like the lonely objects
no one preserves – tweezers
used to pluck
the lightest of chicken feathers
for the Passover meal; the wine cup
leaning to the left from a knock
to the ground. Unclip those Ethafoam
earrings. Use them as buffers, stabilisers.
Become stable. Realise you do not need
to preserve everything.
Flap your Corflute wings. Unstitch
the light. Let it flow

to where it wants to go. Watch
it peer through the crack
in the inpatient's dark painting. Listen
to this crack of light. Wonder
how you could have ever wrapped
it away in the first place. Tear
strips from your calico dress, enclose
this memory-thought gently inside blue
board shoes. Preserve
so you don't forget. Bury in a light-
filled place.

On Photographing Poets

Some poets move too quickly to capture.
Ephemeral creatures, movements traced
in paint-stroke blurs.

I am conscious not to puncture the poem
with the shutter click. Wait for the poet's voice
to cloak me.

My language is no longer words,
but expressions gestures glances –
my hands filling with the music of light.

How to Reawaken a Room

It's a sensory thing. Some rooms soar me light, twirl me west. As though each morning, walls have shifted towards sun, like plants. I drink up rooms' energy. Some rooms are steeped in memory, ritual, learning. You feel it in the air, smell it in the chalk dust and old books. And you are about to enter a חדר.

חדר is Hebrew for Cheder: English translation = room. A learning space for Jewish children. How to reawaken a room? Go back seven years after your Bat Mitzvah. Pegs grip twine. Remember finger-painting the Hebrew letter א. Choosing the windowsill for drying. Watching your work blow out the window – journeying its way down Brisbane city streets.

Visit when no חדר classes are running. Photograph the furniture and chairs covered in carvings and graffiti by Sunday school children across generations: names and dates, Magen Davids and hearts. The smell of old books, drawings and messages that say rooms can be reawakened. Ingredients: an anxious photographer let in by the caretaker with a long memory.

I do not have a long memory. My memory is fragmented; each shard has a single long edge, like a scalene triangle, no sides equal in length. I traverse these longer edges. I walk along them as far as they will let me, always leading me back to the same point and images until I have to make new triangles. My brain looks like an Escher map. Of kitchen tiles. The kitchen is where most memories occur. The touch of a ripe plum from a fruit bowl; cool orange juice on hot days; making heirloom recipes with the matriarch; passing down matzah ball recipes, like a fistful of keys. Kneading keys into challah.

Shlissel Challah

I don't have all the ingredients
to make Shlissel Challah
on the first Shabbat after Passover;
a challah baked
in a key's
shape, to turn
blessings upon
our home.
Baker's yeast –
unavailable
during
pandemic
times. Instead
I knead flour
with vanilla,
sugar, oil, egg.
Roll three strands
to braid into the *stem*.
A circular donut for the *bow*.
A prong for the *bit*. I do not bake
a key inside. Instead, I make a second
challah, bury toffee-coloured dates, brush
with egg, sugar-sprinkled. While it bakes
at 170 degrees for half an hour, I make
challah a third time over with words.
This time, I leave a key.

Mother-daughter Trip

Nana B and Zeide skated
on a lake in Poland's Carpathian Mountains.
I was made for Poland, says Mum, as Brisbane roils
with heat. But we are not headed
for my great-grandparents' homeland;
we are journeying to Geelong.

Mother-daughter trips are good for the soul,
says my shrink. *Don't talk to any strange men,*
says Dad. It's the first time Mum's travelled
without Dad since their 1981 wedding –
seven hours by taxi plane shuttle bus train.
We could have flown to Japan.

Our sense of direction is legendary
for leading us astray.

We
walk
down

       the
       same
       street

             three
             times

Do you recognise where we are?
I was born for the Shtetl.
I imagine her in a small Eastern
European village deep
in history's memory,
a train ride away from the ice-
skating lake. I see

pathways requiring no compass or map;
see her dancing from rooftops with Chagall,
green donkeys, violins.

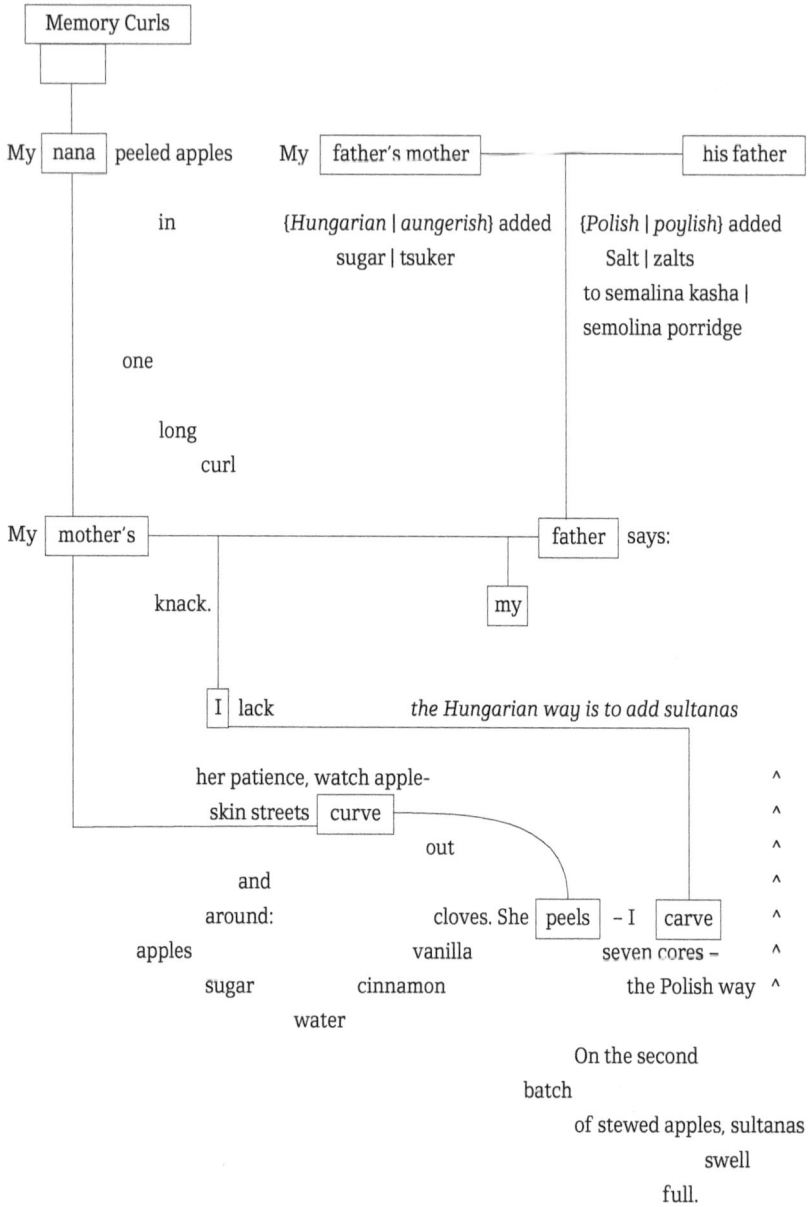

Memory Curls

My [nana] peeled apples   My [father's mother]———————[his father]

                in   {*Hungarian* | *aungerish*} added   {*Polish* | *poylish*} added
                            sugar | tsuker   Salt | zalts
                                                                   to semalina kasha |
                                                                   semolina porridge

        one

            long
                curl

My [mother's]————————————————————[father] says:

        knack.   [my]

            [I] lack   *the Hungarian way is to add sultanas*

        her patience, watch apple-   ^
            skin streets [curve]———————   ^
                            out   ^
        and   ^
        around: cloves. She [peels] – I [carve]   ^
    apples   vanilla   seven cores –   ^
        sugar   cinnamon   the Polish way ^
            water

                                    On the second
                                batch
                                    of stewed apples, sultanas
                                                swell
                                        full.

Of Matriarchs, Work, and Wishes

In sewing boxes: buttons in medicine bottles,
thimbles, bra hooks and old suspender straps.
Nana's initials from before she married: A.B.
Her mother found work as a machinist
during the Depression. Pregnant
with her second girl, she created a disguise –
padded herself with pillows like a Passover
matzah ball. Seven months on she fainted
at the machine, lost her job.

Nana remembers the frilly dresses her mother made
from nighties. Her mother worked from home, trying
to please difficult women – afterwards refused
to teach her girls to sew. Now I stitch
buttons onto cardigans, patch
tears in clothes with findings from my great
grandmother's wooden sewing boxes. Buried
under antique lace – a silver wishbone wrapped
in thread.

Typing Nana's Story

We sit at the computer. Her fingers
type in the correct position – slow perfect
precision, except for her pointer and ring
fingers seized up. I can see her trying to push
past the multiple sclerosis, to expel
it from her being.

Next time I visit, her hands are clawed – don't
press well so I offer to type. She glows
with brilliant sounding paragraphs, intimate
details. I try to capture it all, fingers skate
over keys to keep the magic of her words. I don't
want to tell her to stop, so I push
myself to catch each phrase, each story.

Her musical dictation plunges
me into the scene. At school her friends
called her the Polish princess. Now
she is a regal queen, and I her loyal
subject. The keyboard electric
with her tale – last week it was escaping
the pogroms in Poland. This week –
the final paragraph. She writes the *Shema*,
a parting prayer.

And there's this feeling of completion. She has left
her legacy, for generations to come. I hug
her through the arms of the wheelchair, sinking
into soft skin, breathing
in her scent.

I wheel her to her room. Her paintings dance
on walls: oils and charcoals. Abstracts
in watercolours and Indian ink. Carved
candlesticks illuminate a Shabbat dinner, fire
becomes spirit. Forever an artist, forever
my queen, forever a Polish princess.

A Box of Cadbury Roses

Grandad startles awake when we whisper.
Well hello, isn't this marvellous. We show
him the silver box and he grins
with all his teeth.

He chooses a peppermint cream
and a hazelnut whirl, sucks
out the middle and chomps –
we hear every bite. *Don't watch.*
We gaze at him eat. Coloured twist-
wrappers confetti the table.
These won't see tomorrow.

He dips his hand into the box and finds
a vanilla butter caramel. *Cadbury Roses
were your favourite*, says Mum.
You used to bring them home from work.
He doesn't answer. His eyes are closed,
the taste of a memory just beyond
his reach.

Festive Meal

I chop the egg with a knife, pour
saltwater. We can't find
the table salt, so Mum magicks
flakes from the seven seas. We eat
the egg with silver teaspoons, unwrapped
from their cellophane. Gifts
from my mother's mother and father,
for their wedding. Mum asks
me to keep the cellophane.

I scoop the gefilte fish, place
a piece of orange carrot on top – tradition
so strong, carrot and fish are bottled
in the same glass jar. Red
horseradish is passed
from person to person.

Matzah dumpling in bowls
of chicken soup. Light
and fluffy, ginger-
spiced. I am too full
for lamb curry, spoon
five pieces onto my plate. Save
room for Passover cake; apple and almond
from the Monday Morning
Cooking Club recipe. *Reminds me*
of Nana's Passover cakes, says Dad.
High praise.

Shul | שול | is Yiddish for Synagogue. Yahrzeit | יארצייט | is the Jewish anniversary of a loved one's death. Shavuot | שבועות | is a festival of harvest, celebration, and joy.

Shul with My Mother

We are moving and fast forwarding and rewinding and standing in Shul. Standing and sitting. I am too self-conscious to speak the Hebrew aloud. I hear my mother sing. I hold this memory in a place of melody: my mother sits in her mother's and grandmother's seat. I sit in my mother's seat. On the other side of Shul my three great-aunts once sang. Below the women's balconies – the men. This is a place of memory, prayer. Tonight is Shavuot, Nana's yahrzeit and my great-grandmother's yahrzeit – the reason we are here. After the service my mother sits for moments longer. I ask if she is okay – want to know what she was thinking and feeling when her eyes were closed. She says she felt her mother and grandmother were in Shul in the seat where they once sat. The Shul's round stained-glass windows are pushed open – wide enough for visiting spirits to slip through like a *coda*: a parallel gift.

Notes

'People Die in Seclusion Rooms': This poem references news reports from 2017 about Miriam Merten who died in a seclusion room in an Australian psychiatric hospital in 2014 and references my own experiences from 2011.

'Ingredients for Preservation': Calico, Blue board, Corflute, Mylar, Ethafoam, and Tyvek, are often used in museums and galleries as materials for preservation.

'Mother-daughter Trip': *Shtetl* is Yiddish for 'town'. In Eastern Europe, these small villages had large Jewish populations before the Holocaust. Families would often live in the same Shtetl for generations.

Acknowledgements

This book was written in Meanjin (Brisbane). I acknowledge the traditional custodians of the land – the Jagera and Turrbal people, and pay my respects to Elders past and present.

Thank you to the editors of *Cordite Poetry Review*, *Chicago Quarterly Review* (Australian Writers Anthology), *Westerly*, *Rabbit Journal*, *Griffith Review*, *Neptune: A Dream Archive* (COVID-19 Collective Dream Journal), the *Writing with Water* chapbook (Red Room Poetry), the Red Room Poetry Fellowship Shortlist Commission, *Arts Access Australia 2020 Meeting Place online magazine*, *Bramble Journal*, *Admissions* (Upswell, 2022), *Blue Bottle Journal*, *Heroine's Anthology Vol. 2*, *Verity La*, *Visual Verse*, *Urinal Mag*, and *Small Packages*, where poems from my collection first appeared.

My poem 'Grounding Techniques' was first screened as a recording as part of the Wheeler Centre's 'Writing the Future of Health' performance through The Big Anxiety Festival. 'Memory Curls' was shortlisted in the Woollahra Digital Literary Award (Poetry). My poem 'Festive Meal' premiered in my video art, commissioned by Museum of Brisbane as part of an Artists @ Home Residency in 2020. A version of my drawing 'Self-portrait While Depressed' from my poem 'One of These Scenes is Not Real' was a finalist in the Marie Ellis Prize for Drawing.

Thank you to the incredible Felicity Plunkett for mentoring me on this project. This project has been assisted by the Australian Government through the Australia Council for the Arts, its arts funding and advisory body through the Resilience Create Fund. This project has also been assisted by a Queensland Writers Fellowship. The Queensland Writers Fellowships are supported by the Queensland Government through Arts Queensland, and State Library of Queensland. I am grateful to the wonderful Terri-ann White from Upswell, for publishing my book.

Finally, thank you to my supportive family and friends. Thank you, Mum, and Dad, I am grateful you let me capture our stories together and special thanks to my brother, Alan, to whom this collection is dedicated and who inspired the title poem and many others – my collection *Anxious in a Sweet Store* could not be without you.

About Upswell

Upswell Publishing was established in 2021 by Terri-ann White as a not-for-profit press. A perceived gap in the market for distinctive literary works in fiction, poetry and narrative non-fiction was the motivation. In her years as a bookseller, writer and then publisher, Terri-ann has maintained a watch on literary books and the way they insinuate themselves into a cultural space and are then located within our literary and cultural inheritance. She is interested in making books to last: books with the potential to still be noticed, and noted, after decades and thus be ripe to influence new literary histories.

About this typeface

Book designer Becky Chilcott chose Foundry Origin not only as a strong, carefully considered, and dependable typeface, but also to honour her late friend and mentor, type designer Freda Sack, who oversaw the project. Designed by Freda's long-standing colleague, Stuart de Rozario, much like Upswell Publishing, Foundry Origin was created out of the desire to say something new.

www.ingramcontent.com/pod-product-compliance
Lightning Source LLC
Chambersburg PA
CBHW030848090426
42737CB00009B/1144